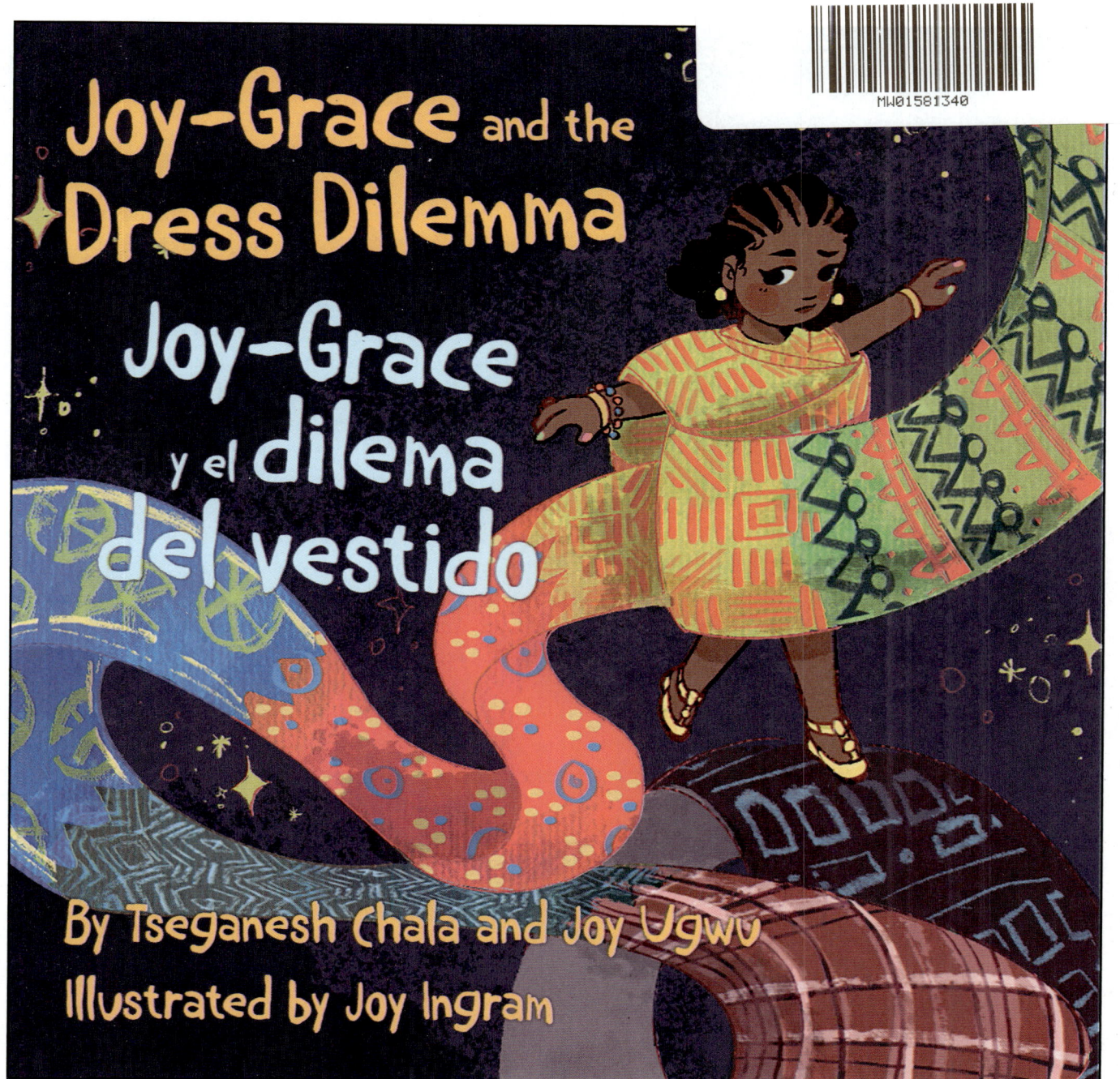

Joy-Grace and the Dress Dilemma
Joy-Grace y el dilema del vestido

By Tseganesh Chala and Joy Ugwu

Illustrated by Joy Ingram

Latin American Youth Center | Washington, DC

Shout Mouse Press

Latin American Youth Center/
Shout Mouse Press

Text copyright © 2021
by Shout Mouse Press

Illustrations copyright © 2021
by Joy Ingram

Design by Amber Colleran

Spanish translation by
Tatiana Figueroa Ramirez
and Ártemis López

ISBN: 978-1-950807-39-0

Shout Mouse Press is a nonprofit writing and publishing program dedicated to amplifying underheard voices. Learn more and see our full catalog at www.shoutmousepress.org.

Shout Mouse Press
1638 R Street NW Suite 218
Washington, DC 20009

Trade distribution:
Ingram Book Group

For information about special discounts and bulk purchases, please contact Shout Mouse Press sales at 240-772-1545 or orders@shoutmousepress.org.

Shout Mouse Press supports copyright. Copyright fuels creativity, encourages diverse voices, promotes free speech, and creates a vibrant culture. Thank you for buying an authorized edition of this book and for complying with copyright laws by not reproducing, scanning, or distributing any part of it in any form without permission. You are supporting writers and allowing Shout Mouse to continue to publish books for every reader.

Today At Apple is a registered trademark of Apple Inc.

Acknowledgments

At Shout Mouse Press, we invite young people to write diverse and inclusive stories inspired by their own lived experiences. We believe that all children should be able to see themselves in the books they read, and that all children benefit from reading diverse perspectives on our shared world.

This book, written by young people from the Latin American Youth Center in Washington, DC, is born of this mission. These youth authors, ages 16-22, worked in teams of two to four to compose original children's books centering the hopes, dreams, joys, and challenges of being a young immigrant. They put their own hearts—and their personalities!—on the page, writing stories they hoped would inspire young readers to embrace who they are and to value the unique stories each one of us has to tell. These authors have our immense gratitude and respect: Mario, Jamileth, Tseganesh, Joy, Deyssy, Yenner, Andy, Marisol, Pedro, and Yunior.

This project represents a collaboration between Shout Mouse Press and the Latin American Youth Center (LAYC). From LAYC: Thanks to Cheili Obregon-Molina and Arisleidy Aquino for essential translation, collaboration, and positive energy, and to the LAYC program leadership of Julia Kann and Mike Leon. From Shout Mouse Press: We thank Programs Manager Alexa Patrick; Story Coaches Faith Campbell, Tatiana Figueroa Ramirez, and Barrett Smith; and Author Liaisons Rosa Reyes, Saylenis Palmore, Josselyn Mendoza, and Brenda Romero Peña for bringing fun and insight to the project. We can't thank enough illustrators Joy Ingram, Yurieli Otero-Asmar, Fatima Seck, and Ian Springer for bringing these stories to life with their beautiful artwork, and Amber Colleran for bringing a keen eye and important mentorship to the project as the series Art Director. Also muchísimas gracias are in order for Tatiana Figueroa Ramirez and Ártemis López for their thoughtful translation. We are grateful for the time and talents of these writers, mentors, and artists!

Finally, we are grateful to Today At Apple® Creative Studios DC, whose support made this project possible.

To all the multicultural kids who feel like their background is confusing or different. Embrace all the unique parts of you that make you, you!

A todos los niños multiculturales que sienten que sus orígenes son confusos y diferentes. ¡Acepta todas tus partes únicas que te hacen ser quien eres!

My name is Joy-Grace, and I'm a fashionista. I love pink and yellow and poufs and glitter. All of my friends know me for my bright colorful dresses. Look at my signature twirl!

Me llamo Joy-Grace y soy una fashionista. Me encantan el rosa, el amarillo, los pufs y los brillos. Todos mis amigos me conocen por mis vestidos de colores brillantes. ¡Mira qué bien giro!

This week at school we have Culture Day. To celebrate, we all have to bring in something to represent our culture.

My friend Pablo says, "I'm bringing my mother's *cantarito* from Guatemala."

My friend Lisa says, "I'm bringing my uncle's bagpipe from Ireland."

My friend Georgia is from the South. "I'm bringing my grandmother's peach cobbler. What about you?"

I put my hands on my hips. "I'm bringing a dress, of course!"

Esta semana en la escuela tenemos el Día de la Cultura. Para celebrar, todos tenemos que llevar algo que represente nuestra cultura.

—Voy a traer el cantarito de mi madre de Guatemala —dice mi amigo Pablo.

—Voy a traer la gaita de mi tío de Irlanda —dice mi amiga Lisa.

—Voy a traer el pastel de durazno de mi abuela. ¿Y tú? —pregunta mi amiga Georgia, que es del sur.

Me pongo las manos en mis caderas:

—¡Traeré un vestido, por supuesto!

But what dress represents "my culture"?

My mom is from Nigeria.
My dad is from Ethiopia.
I was born in Jamaica.
And I've lived in America pretty much all my life.

So…. how can I choose?

Pero, ¿qué vestido representa "mi cultura"?

Mi mamá es de Nigeria.
Mi papá es de Etiopía.
Yo nací en Jamaica.
Y he vivido en los Estados Unidos prácticamente toda mi vida.

Entonces… ¿Cómo puedo elegir?

When my sister picks me up, I tell her about my dilemma.

"I remember when I had to do that. Maybe you can bring one of the quadrille dresses I sell."

My sister knows a lot about Jamaica. She lived there for ten years. She and my dad still go back all the time to sing at my dad's church.

Cuando mi hermana me recoge, le cuento mi dilema.

—Recuerdo cuando tuve que hacer eso. Tal vez puedas traer uno de los vestidos de cuadrilla que vendo.

Mi hermana sabe mucho sobre Jamaica. Vivió allí durante diez años. Ella y mi papá todavía vuelven a con frecuencia para cantar en la iglesia de mi papá.

She hands me a quadrille dress from her work bag. I look at the red criss-cross pattern. It reminds me of the market in Jamaica, where vendors sold bright fabrics and gospel music filled the air. I can almost smell the scent of Jamaican beef patties and fresh mangoes.

OK, a Jamaican dress feels right. Mi 'ave it!

Me pasa un vestido de cuadrilla de su bolso de trabajo. Miro el patrón rojo entrecruzado. Me recuerda al mercado de Jamaica, donde los vendedores vendían telas brillantes y la música evangélica llenaba el aire. Casi puedo oler el aroma de las empanadas de carne de Jamaica y los mangos frescos.

Está bien, un vestido jamaicano me parece correcto. ¡Mi 'ave it!

When I walk in the house, I'm bursting with excitement. I smell fresh tomatoes, maggi, and peppers. My grandmother is humming. The melody is accented by the *pop pop* of the onions and the *shhzz* of the goat meat in the hot oil.

I run into the kitchen. "Nne Oche, check out my dress!"

Cuando entro a la casa, estoy llena de emoción. Huelo tomates frescos, maggi y pimientos. Mi abuela tararea. El *pop pop* de las cebollas y el *shhzz* de la carne de cabra en el aceite caliente se combinan con la música.

Corro a la cocina.

—Nne Oche, ¡mira mi vestido!

My grandmother looks at me. "Good afternoon to you too." She sucks her teeth and laughs.

"Oh sorry, Nne Oche. Good afternoon."

"Dalu, my dear? Why are you so excited?"

I tell her about my Culture Day project.

Mi abuela me mira.

—Buenas tardes a ti también —chasquea la lengua y se ríe.

—Oh, lo siento, Nne Oche. Buenas tardes.

—¿Dalu, querida? ¿Por qué estás tan emocionada?

Le hablo de mi proyecto del Día de la Cultura.

"A Jamaican dress? But why don't you bring the dress from your Uncle's wedding?" Nne Oche made me a beautiful Nigerian dress called akwa omuma for the festivities. I remember running around with my cousins and putting dollar bills on the bride's forehead. It was so much fun!

OK, a Nigerian dress seems right. Enwetera m ya!

—¿Un vestido jamaicano? ¿Pero por qué no llevas el vestido de la boda de tu tío? —Nne Oche me hizo un hermoso vestido nigeriano llamado akwa omuma para las festividades. Recuerdo que corría con mis primos y ponía billetes de dólares en la frente de la novia. ¡Fue tan divertido!

Está bien, un vestido nigeriano me parece correcto. ¡Enwetera m ya!

I hear a *knock knock* at the door and realize that my Ethiopian Grandma has just arrived for dinner. She joins us every Monday for a family meal. I run and jump to embrace her. Ayate smiles and hugs me tightly. She puts me down and kisses me three times on each of my cheeks.

Oigo como alguien llama a la puerta y me doy cuenta de que mi abuela etíope acaba de llegar para la cena. Ella nos acompaña todos los lunes para una comida en familia. Corro y salto para abrazarla. Ayate sonríe y me abraza con fuerza. Me baja y me besa tres veces en cada una de mis mejillas.

I tell her about my Culture Day project and show her my Nigerian dress.

"What about the tibeb I got you when I went to Ethiopia? Remember? I had it made special for you by the shamani." I wore it for Addis Amet, Ethiopian New Year. All of my friends came over to celebrate. We ate doro wot and they all admired my dress.

OK, an Ethiopian dress seems right. Agenyehu!

Le digo de mi proyecto para el Día de la Cultura y le muestro mi vestido nigeriano.

—¿Y el tibeb que te conseguí cuando fui a Etiopía? ¿Te acuerdas? Lo mandé a hacer especialmente para ti por el shamani.

Me lo puse para Addis Amet, el año nuevo etíope. Todos mis amigos vinieron a celebrar. Comimos doro wot y todos admiraron mi vestido.

Está bien, un vestido etíope me parece correcto. ¡Agenyehu!

When we sit down for dinner, I'm wearing my tibeb.

"How do I look, everyone?" I do my signature twirl and put my hands on my hips. "This is what I'm wearing for Culture Day."

"Don't wear that to dinner," my mom says, "you're going to get it dirty."

Nne Oche looks confused and upset. "Mba! No! What about the dress I gave you?"

My sister whips her head toward me. "Eey? What about my quadrille dress?!"

Cuando nos sentamos a cenar, llevo puesto mi tibeb.

—¿Cómo me ven? —hago mi giro característico y me pongo las manos en las caderas— Esto es lo que me voy a poner para el Día de la Cultura.

—No te pongas eso para cenar —dice mi mamá—, vas a ensuciarlo.

Nne Oche parece confundida y molesta:

—¡Mba! ¡No! ¿Y el vestido que te di?

Mi hermana mueve la cabeza hacia mí:

—¿Eey? ¡¿Qué hay de mi vestido de cuadrilla?!

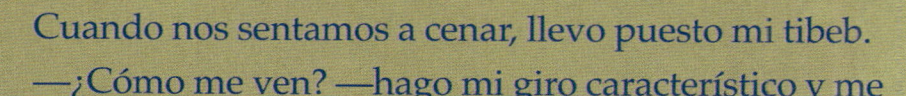

Suddenly everyone's talking at the same time. I shrink down and put my head on the table. Tears drop onto my dress. I don't want everyone to be sad, but I don't know what to wear!

My mom puts her hand on my back. My dad says, "You're the fashionista. You'll figure something out."

De repente, todos están hablando a la vez. Me encojo y pongo la cabeza sobre la mesa. Las lágrimas caen sobre mi vestido. No quiero que todos estén tristes, ¡pero no sé qué ponerme!

Mi mamá me pone la mano en la espalda. Mi papá dice:
—Eres la fashionista. Ya se te ocurrirá algo.

I go to my room, dragging my feet. I throw my tibeb on the bed. They don't get it! I can't just pick one. I don't want to disappoint anybody. I shove the clothes into a pile.

Then I look at the dresses and think, *They kind of go together, in a funny way.*

Voy a mi cuarto arrastrando los pies y tiro mi tibeb sobre la cama. ¡No lo entienden! No puedo elegir uno sin más. No quiero decepcionar a nadie. Pongo la ropa en un montón.

Luego miro los vestidos y pienso, como que combinan, es *muy gracioso*.

I got it!
I grab my pencil case and my design book!
I start to draw. I draw and I draw.
This will be my greatest creation yet!

¡Lo tengo!
¡Agarro mi estuche de lápices y mi libro de diseño! Empiezo a dibujar. Dibujo y dibujo.
¡Esta será mi mayor creación hasta ahora!

Later that night, Nne Oche, Ayate, and my sister help me sew my design. We sew and we sew. We have so much fun working together. Each one brings something unique to our project. I can't wait to see how it all comes together…

Luego esa noche, Nne Oche, Ayate y mi hermana me ayudan a coser mi diseño. Cosemos y cosemos. Nos divertimos tanto trabajando juntas. Cada una aporta algo único a nuestro proyecto. No puedo esperar a ver cómo se junta todo...

Tada! My dress is absolutely beautiful! I do my signature twirl in front of everyone. I'm proud that for Culture Day, I included ALL my cultures. Each one is special! I never have to choose just one.

¡Tachán! ¡Mi vestido es absolutamente hermoso! Hago mi giro característico frente a todos. Me enorgullece que para el Día de la Cultura haya podido incluir TODAS mis culturas. ¡Cada una es especial! Nunca tengo que elegir solo una.

About the Authors

Joy Ugwu is 19 years old and studying at Carnegie Mellon University. She enjoys baking and watching funny videos of her sisters. She was born in Jamaica to Igbo immigrants from Nigeria. When she was two years old she moved with her family from Jamaica to the States. She recalls a family friend calling her "NiJaMaican" referring to her Nigerian-Jamaican-American identity. She wrote this book because she didn't see a lot of African cultures and languages represented. She hopes readers realize they don't have to choose any one of their cultures. It's not a melting pot, it's a mosaic!

Joy Ugwu tiene 19 años y estudia en la Universidad de Carnegie Mellon. Le gusta la repostería y ver vídeos cómicos con sus hermanas. Nació en Jamaica y sus padres son inmigrantes Igbo de Nigeria. Cuando tenía dos años se mudó con su familia de Jamaica a los Estados Unidos. Recuerda cómo una amiga de la familia la llamaba "NiJaMaican" refiriéndose a su identidad Nigeriana-jamaicana-americana. Escribió este libro porque no vio muchas culturas e idiomas africanos representados en libros de niños. Espera que los lectores se den cuenta de que no tienen que escoger una de sus culturas para definir su identidad. No es un crisol cultural, ¡es un mosaico!

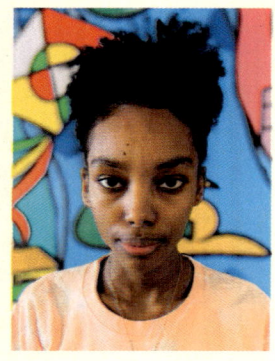

Tseganesh Chala is a senior at Theodore Roosevelt High School. She likes playing soccer and spending time with her friends and family. She is Ethiopian and moved to the United States when she was 16. She comes from a country where people have different cultures and languages: there are more than 80 different ethnic groups in Ethiopia. She wrote this book for all the multicultural children so they can feel proud of who they are and not be afraid or confused to represent their culture.

Tseganesh Chala está en su cuarto año en la escuela secundaria Theodore Roosevelt. Le gusta jugar al fútbol y pasar tiempo con sus amigos y familia. Es etíope y se mudó a los Estados Unidos cuando tenía 16 años. Viene de un país donde la gente tiene muchas culturas e idiomas: hay más de 80 diferentes grupos étnicos en Etiopía. Escribió este libro para todos los niños multiculturales para que se sientan orgullosos de quienes son y para que no tengan miedo o estar confundidos de representar su cultura.

Barrett Smith served as Story Coach for this book, with **Rosa Reyes** supporting.

About the Illustrator

Joy Ingram is a graduate of Virginia Commonwealth University in Richmond. She is interested in portraying stories through art and representing marginalized communities. She loves using bright colors and finds inspiration from her Caribbean American background. She is interested in digital artwork and children's illustration. You can view more of her work at https://www.joyeryart.com/.

Joy Ingram es una graduada de la Universidad de Virginia Commonwealth en Richmond. Ella está interesada en representar historias a través del arte y en representar comunidades marginalizadas. A ella le encanta usar colores brillantes y encuentra inspiración en sus raíces caribeñas. Le interesan el arte digital y la ilustración para niños. Puedes ver más de su trabajo aquí https://www.joyeryart.com/.

Writers and artists at work

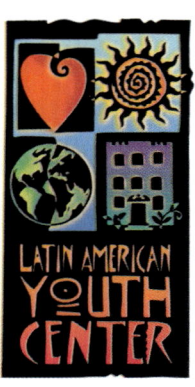

ABOUT LAYC

The Latin American Youth Center (LAYC) is a DC-based nonprofit organization that offers a variety of programming to low-income youth of all backgrounds. Their mission is to empower a diverse population of young people to achieve a successful transition to adulthood, through multicultural, comprehensive, and innovative programs that address youths' social, academic, and career needs.

El Latin American Youth Center (LAYC) es una organización sin fines de lucro con sede en Washington, DC que ofrece una variedad de programas para jóvenes de bajos recursos de todos los orígenes. Su misión consiste en capacitar a una población diversa de jóvenes para que logren una transición exitosa a la edad adulta a través de programas multiculturales, integrales e innovadores que abordan las necesidades sociales, académicas y profesionales de la juventud.

Learn more at layc-dc.org

ABOUT SHOUT MOUSE PRESS

Shout Mouse Press is a nonprofit organization dedicated to centering and amplifying the voices of marginalized youth (ages 12+) via writing workshops, publication, and public speaking opportunities. The young people we coach are underrepresented—as characters and as creators—within young people's literature, and their perspectives underheard. Our work provides a platform for them to tell their own stories and, as published authors, to act as leaders and agents of change.

Shout Mouse Press es una organización sin fines de lucro dedicada a centrar y amplificar las voces de los jóvenes marginalizados (a partir de los 12 años) a través de talleres de escritura, publicación, y oportunidades para hablar en público. La gente joven a la que entrenamos está subrepresentada—como personajes y como creadores—en la literatura para gente joven, y sus perspectivas son poco escuchadas. Nuestro trabajo les proporciona una plataforma para contar sus propias historias y, como autores publicados, actuar como líderes y agentes de cambio.

Learn more at shoutmousepress.org

MORE BOOKS FROM SHOUT MOUSE PRESS

Shout Mouse Press is passionate about letting young people speak for themselves—and making sure they are heard. We lead writing and art workshops that center youth voices, then edit and design their books, and finally publish and promote their important work. We ensure that earned income from book sales is invested directly back into young people themselves: proceeds support scholarship funds for author communities, salaries for author interns, and programs that help young people speak up, be heard, and be taken seriously as leaders in their community.

Check out our catalogue of 50+ award-winning youth-authored titles including children's books, graphic novels, novels, memoirs, and poetry collections at **shoutmousepress.org**.

  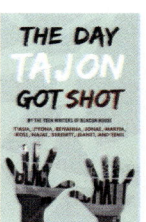 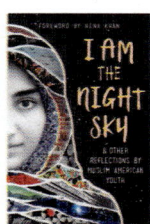 

WHERE TO BUY

We encourage you to order books directly through Shout Mouse Press online in order to best benefit our authors. For bulk orders, educator inquiries, and nonprofit discounts: email **orders@shoutmousepress.org**.

Books are also available through Amazon, Bookshop.org, and other online retailers.

Shout Mouse titles are distributed by Ingram.

OTHER WAYS TO ENGAGE

Shout Mouse Press can bring speakers to your class or event. Call us at 240-772-1545 or request via **shoutmousepress.org/request-an-author-talk**.

Support our youth writing and publishing programs by becoming a donor: **shoutmousepress.org/donate**.

OUR IMPACT

90,000+
Shout Mouse books in circulation

8
National Literary Awards, including 4 Book of the Year Designations

$140,000+
raised in scholarship funds for author communities

20,000+
audience members reached through 100+ Author Talks in schools, libraries, and conferences

20,000+
books donated to young readers in need

SHOUT MOUSE PRESS / LAYC BILINGUAL BOOK SPOTLIGHT:

VOCES SIN FRONTERAS

As immigrants and activists, the Latino Youth Leadership Council of LAYC recognized the urgent need for #OwnVoices stories to provide a human face to the U.S. immigration debate. With few youth-focused books reflecting their personal narratives, they decided to boldly share their own. The Shout Mouse team of teaching artists and comic coaches worked with these youth leaders to share their memoirs about immigrating to the U.S., and now educators across the country are using their stories to educate, affirm, and inspire their students. For ages 12+.

Voces Sin Fronteras: Our Stories, Our Truth
978-1945434921

Voces Sin Fronteras is a bilingual collection of 16 self-illustrated graphic memoirs by teen immigrants from Central America and the Caribbean. These thought-provoking and powerfully honest stories address themes of poverty, family, grief, education, and, of course, the pain and promise of immigration. This book is an opportunity to hear directly from youth who are often in the headlines but whose stories don't get told in full. Foreword by Newbery Medal winner Meg Medina.

"When I tell my story, it heals what it is in my past.... If you never share, the pain will never leave, it will always be there... [Telling your story] will help you to heal inside, to be who you are, to speak out."

— Erminia, co-author of *Voces Sin Fronteras*, on the power of sharing her story via Author Talks

REVIEWS

"This powerful compendium amplifies teens' understanding of the young immigrant experience— facing fears, overcoming sadness, learning a new language, and being left by parents who migrated first, then forgiving and reuniting with them decades later... VERDICT: Spotlighting underrepresented voices, this work is highly recommended for all communities in their efforts to promote empathetic, inclusive discussions around immigration."
—*School Library Journal*, Starred Review

"The compelling stories shared by these students… signal their desire to serve as beacons or lifelines for other young immigrants. Their testimonies, as Newbery Medal winner Meg Medina points out in her foreword, are ultimately about courage… Enlightening and inspiring #ownvoices accounts by young activists."   — Kirkus Reviews

AWARDS

2020 International Latino Book Awards
Best Young Adult Nonfiction

2019 "In the Margins"
Top Nonfiction Prize

Made in the USA
Middletown, DE
01 December 2021